Watch It Grow!

Pan-Canadian
Science Place Team

Gary Cross

Xavier Fazio

Don Kelly

Jo-Anne Lake

Denise MacDonald

Susan Martin

Kathleen Rosborough

Wayne Stewart

Brian Veitch

Barbara Wall

Judy Willson

Scientific Accuracy

Elaine P. Simons
Department of Botany, University of British Columbia

Scholastic Canada Ltd.

Watch It Grow!

LESSON 1   What Are Plants? 4

LESSON 2   How Are Plants Different? .6

LESSON 3   What Do Plants Need? 8

LESSON 4   Why Do Plants Live in Different Places? 10

LESSON 5   How Do Plants Make Food? 12

LESSON 6   Why Do Plants Have Seeds? 14

LESSON 7   How Do Plants Make New Seeds? 16

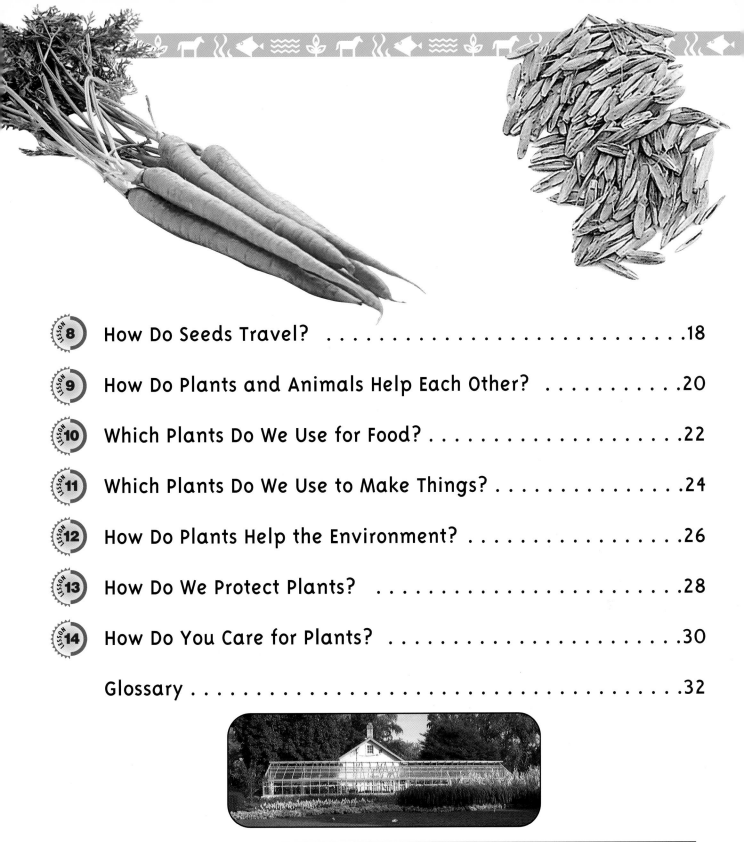

8 How Do Seeds Travel? .18

9 How Do Plants and Animals Help Each Other? 20

10 Which Plants Do We Use for Food? 22

11 Which Plants Do We Use to Make Things? 24

12 How Do Plants Help the Environment? 26

13 How Do We Protect Plants? 28

14 How Do You Care for Plants? 30

Glossary 32

This symbol 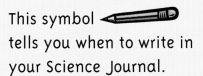 tells you when to write in your Science Journal.

This symbol ⬡ **Be Aware!** shows you when to be careful.

Words in **green** are explained in the glossary on page 32.

What Are Plants?

Plants are living things, like animals. Remember that people and many animals begin as babies, and grow up to become adults. Some animals and all insects begin life as eggs. Plants change and grow too. Have you seen plants like these? How do you think they began? How have they changed?

Take a nature walk.

You need:
• magnifier

1 Look at plants growing near your school. How big are they? How are they similar? How are they different?

2 Look at three different plants closely. Draw and write what you see.

3 What are the different parts of plants? (If you don't know the name of a part, you can draw or describe it.) What do you think the parts are for?

4 How do you think these plants will change in their lifetime? What parts will stay the same? What parts will change?

Be Aware! Don't touch any plants or animals on your nature walk without asking an adult first.

THINK! What do all plants have in common?

How Are Plants Different?

Plants have several things in common. Most plants have stems, leaves, and roots. Some also have flowers and fruit. The diagram shows the main features of a plant. There is really no such thing as a typical plant since plants vary so much.

PARTS OF A PLANT

Flower

Fruit

Leaf

Stem

Roots

Plants can be all different sizes, colours, and shapes. Redwoods are the largest living plants on Earth. Some redwoods are taller than 110 metres high, while some pond plants are only half a millimetre across. How can you tell how tall a tree is?

Measure a tree.

You need:
- craft stick
- tape measure

1 Go outside and choose a tree.

2 Ask a classmate to stand next to the tree.

3 Stretch out your arm and hold the craft stick up in front of you.

4 Move back so that the top of the craft stick lines up with the top of your classmate's head, and the bottom with the bottom of your classmate's feet. (In other words, the craft stick will cover your classmate.)

5 Then move the craft stick up so its bottom is at your classmate's head. Mark the top of the craft stick with your finger, and keep moving it up and counting the number of lengths until the craft stick is at the top of the tree.

6 Measure your classmate's height next to the tree.

7 Multiply your classmate's height by the number of craft sticks it took to reach the top of the tree.

8 Use labelled drawings to record your observations.

THINK!
What do you think are some other features that all plants share?

7

What Do Plants Need?

All living things need certain things to live. Take a look at a houseplant that lives in your classroom or home. Is it healthy? Why is it healthy? What do you think are some of the things that it needs to stay healthy?

Compare plant growth.

You need:
• 2 houseplants (both the same kind)
• dark plastic bag

1 Cover one plant with a dark plastic bag and set it out of the sun.

2 Place the other plant in a warm, bright spot, and water it regularly.

3 Predict what will happen to the plant in the bag.

4 After one week, compare the two plants.

8

What changes did you see in the plants? Why do you think the plant in the bag looks unhealthy? Why is the other plant healthy? What would you do to make the unhealthy plant healthy again?

Plants need some things to live. They need food, water, air, sunlight, and space. Plants get food or nutrients from the soil, water from rain, carbon dioxide from the air, and sunlight from the Sun.

THINK!
Sometimes plants become less healthy or even die if there are too many weeds around them. Why do you think this is so?

How could you test what other things plants need to stay healthy? Develop a plan to test for one factor.

Show your plan to your teacher, and **try it!**

9

Why Do Plants Live in Different Places?

▲ Desert

There are very few places on Earth where there are no plants. Every area has its own special types of plants. Look at the photos below. What are the plants like in each area? Why?

▼ Arctic

All plants need certain things to survive, such as food, water, air, space, and sunlight. But not every place on Earth has a lot of all these things. So plants must adapt to the different environments in order to survive. What are some of the different features of plants that help them survive in different areas? How do you think plants change and adapt?

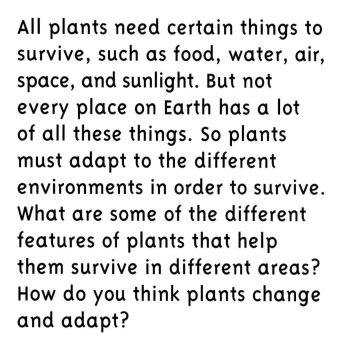

10

▲ Pond

▲ Rainforest

Build a plant maze.

You need:
- shoebox
- cardboard
- scissors
- bean seed
- flowerpot
- pot of soil
- water

1 Cut a hole in one end of a shoebox. Cut two pieces of cardboard to fit inside the box, like shelves. Cut a hole in each piece—one on the right side, and one on the left side.

2 Plant a bean seed (that has soaked in water overnight) in soil. Use a flowerpot small enough to fit inside the bottom third of the shoebox.

Slide the first shelf (with the hole on the right side) into the box. Place the pot on the left side at the bottom of the shoebox.

4 Put the lid on the shoebox, leaving the hole in the top open to the light.

5 Keep the bean watered, and check on it every day or so. After four or five days, what has happened? Why?

When the seed has grown through the first hole, put in the second shelf (with the hole in the left side) about 10 cm above the first shelf. What happens after another four or five days? Why did it happen?

THINK!
What features do plants have to protect them from animals?

Be Aware! Be careful when using scissors to cut the cardboard.

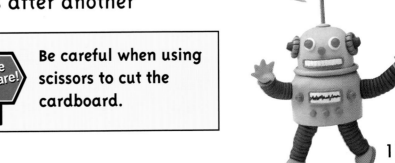

How Do Plants Make Food?

Animals cannot make their own food, but most plants can. Green plants use the carbon dioxide in the air to make the food that helps them grow. How do you think they do this? What do you think plants need besides carbon dioxide to make food?

Watch a plant make food.

You need:
• water plant
• clear jar
• water
• clear bowl
• piece of cardboard

❶ Put the water plant in the jar and fill it to the top with water.

❷ Fill the bowl halfway with water.

❸ Hold the cardboard over the top of the jar and turn it upside down in the bowl of water.

❹ Carefully remove the cardboard, making sure that no air gets in the jar.

❺ Place the bowl and jar in sunlight. What happens? ✎

❻ What do you think the bubbles are made up of? Why do you think they rise to the top of the jar? ✎

The green leaves contain chlorophyll, which traps the energy from the sunlight. It turns water, nutrients, and carbon dioxide into sugary food.

The leaves take in carbon dioxide from the air through tiny pores—stomata.

While the plant makes its food, it gives out oxygen through the pores in its leaves.

The roots of a plant take up water and nutrients from the soil.

During the day, green plants make their own food—sugar—by using carbon dioxide from the air, water from the soil, and energy from the sunlight. This process is called photosynthesis.

In most plants, leaves are the food factories. The leaves contain a substance called chlorophyll, which gives plants their green colour. But it does something more important. Chlorophyll traps the energy from sunlight so that green plants can make food for themselves, grow, and repair damage.

THINK!
Some plants do not make their own food. Research where they get their food.

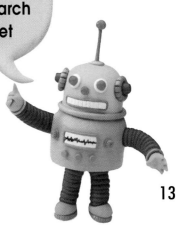

13

Why Do Plants Have Seeds?

Most plants begin life as seeds. Seeds can be many different shapes, sizes, and colours. But the size of a seed doesn't tell you how big the plant will be. The biggest plant on Earth, the redwood tree, starts out as a seed smaller than a dime. Many seeds are foods. If nobody ate them, each seed might grow into the same kind of plant that made it.

What makes a seed grow? Seeds have coats that protect what's inside them. When the soil is warm and wet enough, the seeds begin to change. What changes are happening here?

▲ Germinated seed

Middle stage ▶ of growth (young seedling)

Early ▶ signs of stem and roots

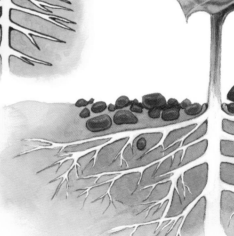

◀ Full-grown sunflower

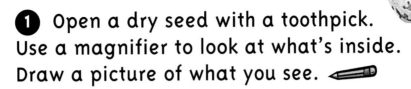

Be a seed scientist.

1 Open a dry seed with a toothpick. Use a magnifier to look at what's inside. Draw a picture of what you see.

2 Soak a paper towel and put it in a plastic bag with five dry seeds. Close the bag so that it stays wet inside. Let it sit for two to three days.

You need:
- lima beans
- toothpick
- magnifier
- paper towel
- water
- plastic bag
- clear cup
- soil

Be Aware! Toothpick ends are sharp!

3 Take a seed from your bag and take it apart with a toothpick. Draw a picture of it next to the drawing of the dry seed. How is it different from the inside of the dry seed?

4 Plant two of the seeds from the bag in a cup of soil. Put the cup in a sunny place. Check it every day.

5 Every two days, remove another seed from your bag. How is the inside of each seed different? Record the changes you see.

What causes a seed to grow? If a seed has water, air, and warmth, it will begin to grow or germinate. Then the seed will begin to grow into a plant. Do you think seeds will grow in the dark?

THINK! How many ways can you group seeds?

How Do Plants Make New Seeds?

Many plants grow flowers. Flowers grow fruit that holds new seeds. Flowers are made up of many parts. What do you think each part is for?

Make a flower model.

You need:
• construction paper
• scissors
• glue
• modelling clay
• pipe cleaners
• baking powder

1 Draw four big **petals** on the construction paper. Cut them out and glue them together. Put a ball of modelling clay at the bottom of your flower.

2 Use a coloured pipe cleaner to make the pistil and four white pipe cleaners to make the stamens.

3 Put baking powder on the top of each stamen. Now gently shake your flower. What happens?

4 What do you think each plant part does?

Before a seed can grow, some pollen from the stamens must land on a pistil of the same kind of flower. This is called pollination.

How do you think pollen gets to a plant's pistil? Often, the wind carries the pollen from the stamens to the pistil. Insects such as bees and butterflies, as well as hummingbirds, help to pollinate, too. When they fly from flower to flower, the pollen rubs onto their bodies. Then they carry the pollen to the next flower, where it rubs off onto the pistil.

When a flower is pollinated, seeds begin to grow inside the pistil. As the seeds grow larger, the pistil ripens into a fruit or pod. It breaks open and the seeds are ready to become new plants.

THINK!
How is a plant's life cycle the same and different from an animal's life cycle?

PARTS OF A FLOWER

Pistil—the female part, where seeds form

Stamen—
the male part,
where the
powder called
pollen forms

Petal

Stem

How Do Seeds Travel?

Many plants die after they make new seeds. So how do their life cycles continue? Some of the plant's seeds fall to the ground near the base of the parent plant, but often, there is not enough room for a new plant to grow. Seeds can continue the life cycle if they have space to grow. This means that many seeds must travel in order to survive. How do you think seeds travel? Do you help seeds travel? How?

Help seeds travel.

You need:
- pair of large wool socks
- tweezers
- magnifier

1 Put the socks on over your shoes.

2 Walk around a grassy area. As you walk, try to brush against plants such as dandelions and burdocks so that seeds stick to the socks.

3 Remove the seeds with tweezers.

4 Examine the seeds with a magnifier. How many different kinds of seeds did you get? Can you guess which seeds came from which plants?

5 What do you think helped these seeds travel?

Wind, water, birds, animals, and people help seeds travel. The wind can carry seeds far away. Some seeds fall into streams, ponds, rivers, or oceans, and are carried to different areas.

Other seeds travel by attaching themselves to people's clothes and animal fur. Birds can drop seeds. Animals, like squirrels, can bury seeds or nuts to eat them later in the winter. Sometimes they forget where they left some of these seeds, and they end up sprouting into new plants in the spring.

THINK!
What are some of the features that help seeds travel?

How Do Plants and Animals Help Each Other?

Plants and animals are a great team. They help each other in many ways. Plants and animals breathe different gases in order to survive. What gas do plants need? Where do they get it?

About 200 years ago, a scientist named Joseph Priestley performed some experiments to find out.

Observe Priestley's experiment.

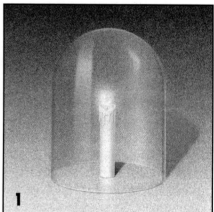

Look at picture 1. Priestley covered a lighted candle with a glass jar. After a few seconds, the flame went out. Fire needs oxygen to burn. Why do you think the flame went out? ✐

Look at picture 2. Priestley put a plant under the jar for 10 days. Then he lit the candle. The flame burned longer than it did without the plant. Why do you think the plant made a difference? ✐

Look at picture 3. Priestley put a live mouse under the jar with the plant. The mouse and the plant stayed alive. What do a mouse and flame both need? What does a plant need? ✐

What do you think Priestley learned about plants and animals from his experiment? ✐

As plants grow, they produce oxygen. Animals breathe the oxygen and give off carbon dioxide. That's where the plants come in again, because plants need carbon dioxide to survive.

THINK!
What other ways do plants and animals depend on each other?

Which Plants Do We Use for Food?

All of the food we eat comes from plants in one way or another. We either eat the plant itself (like carrots, potatoes, cherries, or wheat) or an animal that feeds on plants (such as fish, cows, or chickens). Can you name some plants that we use for food? What plants do you bring to school for lunch?

Grow your own food.

1 Add half a teaspoon or so of seeds and a tablespoon of water to the glass jar. Put the lid on the jar and lay it down on its side in the refrigerator.

2 Check the seeds every day. Make sure that the inside of the jar has many water droplets on it. If it doesn't have many drops, add more water.

You need:
- clean, clear jar with lid
- watercress or alfalfa seeds
- water
- refrigerator

3 What happens to the seeds after a couple of days?

4 Enjoy the sprouts for lunch on a sandwich or in a salad. What part of the plant did you eat?

22

We eat different parts of different plants: flowers, stems, leaves, seeds, roots, and buds. Can you name some foods that come from these plant parts?

THINK!
What part of a plant do you think a potato is?

Which Plants Do We Use to Make Things?

People and animals use plants for many things besides food. Birds use twigs and pieces of grass to build their nests, and people use trees for timber to build their houses and make furniture. Can you think of other things that people use plants for?

◄ What plant parts were used to make this nest?

There are many things that are made out of plants that we use every day. Cotton, rubber, cork, rope, cord, wood, and paper all come from plants. Do you know what plants they come from? What parts of the plant? What can you make out of these things?

Can you identify the ▶ plants that were used in these things?

Make dye from plants.

You need:
- apron
- rubber gloves
- container
- hot water
- 500 g blueberries, beets, or goldenrod
- cotton
- wooden spoon

1 Put on the apron and rubber gloves.

2 Choose berries, beets, or goldenrod. After rinsing them, put them into a container to crush them. Cover them with hot water. Let them sit overnight. Then remove the berries, beets, or goldenrod from the container and put them in a composter.

Put the cotton in the pot. You can let it soak for several hours or even days. What happens to the cotton?

4 When the cotton reaches the colour you want, lift the cotton out with the wooden spoon. Remember that it will look darker than it actually is, because it is wet. Wring out any extra dye, and then wash and rinse the cotton.

What other plants or plant parts could you use to make dyes?

THINK!
There are many people who do work that depends on plants. What are some careers or jobs that depend on plants?

Be Aware! Be careful of the hot water.

How Do Plants Help the Environment?

Have you ever walked on a path through a vacant lot or a park? Maybe other people have been using the same path. What do you notice about the grass and soil along the path?

Have you ever passed a construction site after a heavy rainfall? What happened to the dirt? The soil turns to mud, and with enough rain and no barriers such as plants, it will flow downhill. Large mudslides are like rivers of mud flowing downhill. They can destroy homes, roads, and whole environments. Huge piles of mud can block rivers and streams, creating floods that cause even more damage. Without plants to hold soil in place, the dirt is washed away. How do you think plants hold dirt in place?

When the rain drenches your lawn, you do not have to worry about mudslides or erosion, because the roots of the grass hold the topsoil in place.

How would grass or other ▶ plants help prevent more erosion?

▼ A mudslide in British Columbia causes damage to plants and people.

▲ Grass keeps this hill from turning into mud.

THINK!
One tree farm has five-year-old trees. Another has one-year-old trees. Which tree farm would suffer the most erosion during a bad rainstorm? Why?

How Do We Protect Plants?

Today, many of the world's plants are being threatened by the way we live. For example, farmers need land to grow food and to raise farm animals, so they clear the land of trees, wildflowers, and other plants. Other land is cleared to make room for roads, factories, and houses. Loggers cut down trees for wood used in making houses, furniture, and paper.

For many years, more trees were cut down than could grow back. Something had to be done. Lumber companies and governments began to plant new trees. Other plants need protecting, too.

Special parks have been created to protect the wilderness from logging, farming, development, pollution, and overuse. Now, the trees, flowers, grasses, bushes, lakes, and animals that depend on these plants will be protected and enjoyed for years to come.

What parks in your area protect plants? What are these parks called? What other ways can you protect plants?

▲ Why do you think it is important to plant trees? How can you help?

Plant a flower.

You need:
- flower seeds
- water
- watering can
- flowerpot
- potting soil

1 Plant some flower seeds in a flowerpot. Put the pot in a warm sunny place.

2 Water the pot every few days.

3 Make a chart of your seeds' growth.

4 Compare your chart with a classmate's.

Why are flowers and other plants important to the environment?

THINK!
What do you think would happen if trees were not replanted? Explain your answers.

How Do You Care for Plants?

Have you ever visited a greenhouse in the middle of winter? What did you notice about the plants inside? Plants grow well in greenhouses because the glass walls protect the plants from the cold outdoors but allow the sunlight to enter. What else do plants need to survive in a greenhouse?

Build a terrarium.

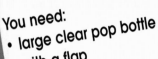

You need:
- large clear pop bottle with a flap
- gravel or small stones
- potting soil
- small plants
- spray bottle or mister
- thermometer

❶ Clean out the bottle and let it dry. Lay it on its side and place a couple of handfuls of gravel on the bottom. What do you think the gravel is for? ✎

❷ On top of the gravel, place a layer 2 cm or more of compost soil and pat it down.

❸ Choose several small plants for your terrarium. Make a small hole to plant each plant. After planting, press the soil down firmly around the plant. Repeat for each plant.

❹ Spray the plants with water from the mister. Place a thermometer in the container so that you can read the temperature easily. Close the flap on the bottle to keep in the moisture.

5 Place the terrarium in a warm, bright spot that is not in direct sunlight.

6 Check your terrarium often. If there aren't any water drops on the inside, mist the plants again. If the inside is completely covered with water drops, open the flap for a few hours or the whole day.

How are the plants doing? You will notice that your miniature garden will grow like one in a greenhouse and will need very little care. Why do you think this is?

How would your model greenhouse have been different if you had not learned about plants in this unit? What were the most important things that you learned in this unit that helped you design a terrarium and care for the plants?

THINK!
How did building a terrarium help you think of and understand things you missed before?

branch
[branch]

A branch is the part of a tree that grows out of the trunk or main part of the tree.

carbon dioxide
[KAR-bun
dye-ok-side]

Carbon dioxide is the part of air that plants need to make food.

flower
[FLOW-ur]

A flower is the part of a plant that grows the fruit or seed.

fruit
[froot]

The part of a plant that contains the seed.

leaf
[leef]

A leaf is the green part growing from a stem or branch. The leaf is where the plant makes its food.

life cycle
[LIFE-SY-kul]

A life cycle is all the changes a plant or animals goes through between birth and death. Every plant has a life cycle.

oxygen
[OK-suh-jin]

The gas that plants and animals breathe in. Plants make oxygen during photosynthesis.

petal
[PET-ul]

A petal is the part of a flower that gives the flower colour and shape.